For Oliver, Graham & Jeremy

Our Water Baby

Written by Amy Maclean
Illustrated by Jan Nesbitt

"It's your birthday," said Oliver's mummy, "and the daffodils are out.

But when the roses flower in the garden,
it will be time for our new baby to be born."

Oliver's mummy was going to have a baby.
For a long time, her tummy had been getting
bigger and bigger and rounder and rounder. "It
looks as if I've swallowed a beach ball!" she said.

"No!" said Oliver. "That's a baby in there.
I can feel the baby moving and waving to me
with his hands and feet!"

Everyone was getting ready for the birth.
Oliver was very excited.
"Will the baby be a boy or a girl?" he wondered.

Oliver's grandparents came to be there to help
look after Oliver.

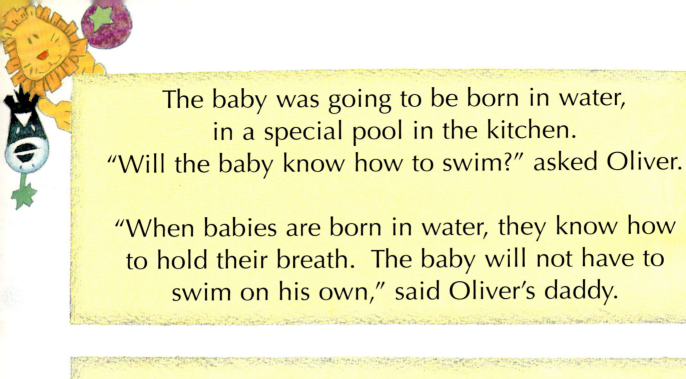

The baby was going to be born in water,
in a special pool in the kitchen.
"Will the baby know how to swim?" asked Oliver.

"When babies are born in water, they know how
to hold their breath. The baby will not have to
swim on his own," said Oliver's daddy.

"That's good," said Oliver. He was relieved.
He loved to swim, but he wouldn't want to
swim on his own!

Together, Oliver and his daddy set up the pool
to see that it worked properly.
They filled it with water just for fun.

Everyone got in and splashed around.
"What fun to have a pool inside," cried Oliver.
"I want the pool to stay here always."

"This is a special pool for the baby's birth,"
replied Mummy, "but when the baby is born,
we can fill the pool in the garden.
We can all go swimming with our new baby."

A few days later, Oliver woke up early.
He heard voices downstairs, so he crept down
to the kitchen. Daddy was filling up the pool
again. Mummy was walking around the kitchen.
"Oliver, today our baby will be born!"

"But will the baby wait for the pool to fill up?"
asked Oliver.

"Yes," answered Daddy. "There is plenty of time
for us to fill the pool before the baby comes."

Mummy was eating toast and moving around on her birth ball. "Why don't you eat your hot cross bun, Oliver? You don't want to be hungry when the baby arrives."

Oliver was so excited that it was hard to eat! Mummy rubbed Oliver's back. He felt very special.

"Why don't we go for a walk, Oliver?" asked Grandad. "You can ride the new bike that you got for your birthday!"

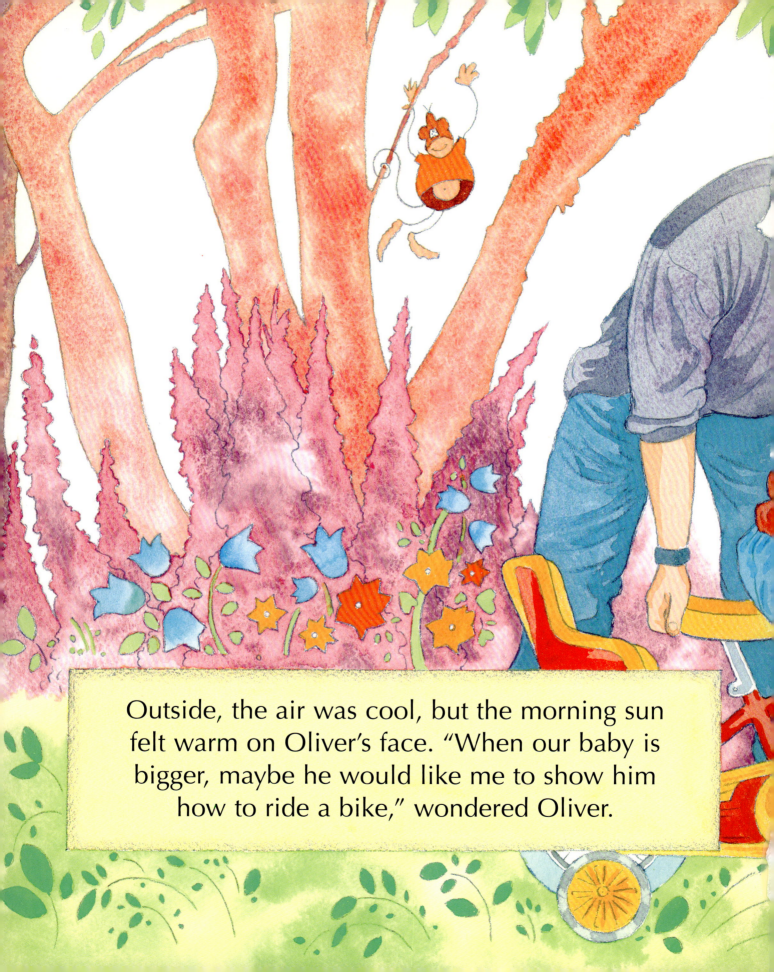

Outside, the air was cool, but the morning sun felt warm on Oliver's face. "When our baby is bigger, maybe he would like me to show him how to ride a bike," wondered Oliver.

"I'm sure the baby will want to learn lots of things from you!" Grandad said.

When Oliver and Grandad returned from their walk, Oliver's mummy was beginning to make long and loud noises. "When a baby is born," explained Oliver's daddy, "it is very hard work for the Mummy. She will get lots of aches and pains. She will feel better when she gets into the pool, and even better when the baby is born."

Oliver's mummy decided to get in the pool.

The water
was warm and deep.

Some of the time
Mummy moved around
in the water and made
lots of noises and splashes.

Then she would lie back
quietly for a while.

Oliver and Grandma watched as
Midwife Sarah listened to the baby's heart.
Her special machine worked underwater!
B-dum, b-dum, b-dum, b-dum!
Oliver could hear the baby's heart
loud and clear.
"That's good," said Sarah.

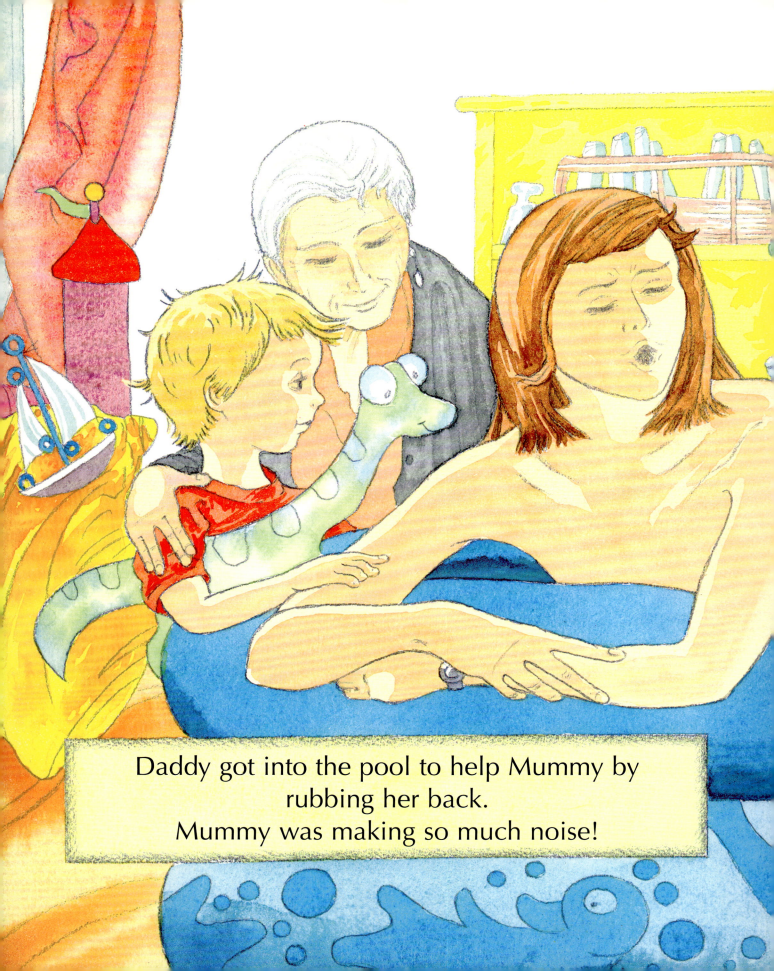

Daddy got into the pool to help Mummy by rubbing her back.
Mummy was making so much noise!

"You are doing so well," praised Daddy.
"It won't be long now. You're doing brilliantly!"
said Sarah. Oliver couldn't wait!
The baby would be born very soon.

"I can feel the baby's head," cried Mummy.
As the baby came out, Daddy caught the baby
and lifted him up. The baby's hands came out
of the water first—then his little face.
He was reaching for the sky!

Mummy and Daddy were crying and laughing at the same time. Oliver leaned over to touch the new baby.

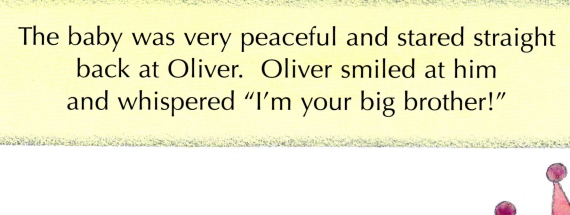

The baby was very peaceful and stared straight
back at Oliver. Oliver smiled at him
and whispered "I'm your big brother!"

After Mummy and Daddy got out of the water, Mummy fed the baby with her special milk.

At last, Oliver got to have his first cuddle with the baby. "I will be very careful," he promised.

He held the baby very gently and looked into the baby's deep dark eyes. "I think he likes me!" Oliver smiled and kissed his new brother.

And just as Mummy had said, that summer they
all swam in the pool in the garden together.